GROW YOUR OWN
Crystal Mini worlds

by the editors of Klutz

KLUTZ

Important SAFETY Information

▶ **This kit is only for use by children over 8 years of age.** Not for use by children under 8 years of age. Store this kit out of reach of young children, and keep young children and pets away from experiments and supplies.

▶ This kit is to be used solely under the strict supervision of adults who have studied the precautions and instructions in the book and packaging.

▶ Read the instructions before use, follow them, and keep them for reference. Save packaging and instructions as they contain important information.

▶ Read and follow these instructions, the safety rules, and the first aid information, and keep them for reference. The incorrect use of chemicals can cause injury and damage to health. Only carry out those activities which are listed in the instructions.

▶ The area surrounding the activity should be kept clear of any obstructions and away from the storage of food. It should be well lit, well ventilated, and close to a water supply. A solid table with a heat-resistant top should be provided.

Please note the following risk and safety information for the substances contained in this kit:

▶ The crystal powder (aluminum potassium sulfate) can cause irritation to your eyes, mouth, and skin. Avoid skin contact with the dry powder or liquid solution.

▶ The dye tablets can stain. Avoid skin contact and protect fabrics and surfaces. The yellow dye contains Yellow #5, which is a known irritant for people with certain sensitivities and allergies.

▶ Eye protection is not included, but is recommended for additional safety precaution.

Advice for parents and supervising adults:

▶ The activities in this book have been designed for children ages 8 and up. However, since children's abilities vary so much, even within age groups, you should review the instructions first and exercise discretion as to which experiments are suitable and safe for them.

▶ The substances and components in this kit have been tested to U.S., Canada, and Australia/New Zealand safety standards. Per these standards, there are no dangerous chemicals included in this kit. However, it is recommended that adults assist in all activities as misuse could result in injury.

▶ Before starting the experiments, your child should carefully read through all the instructions and warnings, and you should discuss the warnings and safety information with your child to make sure they fully understand them. Emphasize to your child the importance of following all instructions and warnings, and the importance of carrying out only those experiments that are described in this book.

First aid information:

▶ **Important:** In case of injury, always seek medical help. Bring the chemical and its packaging with you.

▶ **To contact your local Poison Control Center, please dial:**
   · United States: 1-800-222-1222
   · Canada: 1-416-813-5900
   · New Zealand: 0800 764 766
   · Australia: 13 11 26

▶ **In case of eye contact:** Wash out eye with plenty of water, holding the eye open if necessary. Seek immediate medical help.

▶ **If swallowed:** Do not induce vomiting. Seek immediate medical advice.

▶ For any injuries or adverse reactions, seek medical advice.

CONTENTS

WHAT YOU GET

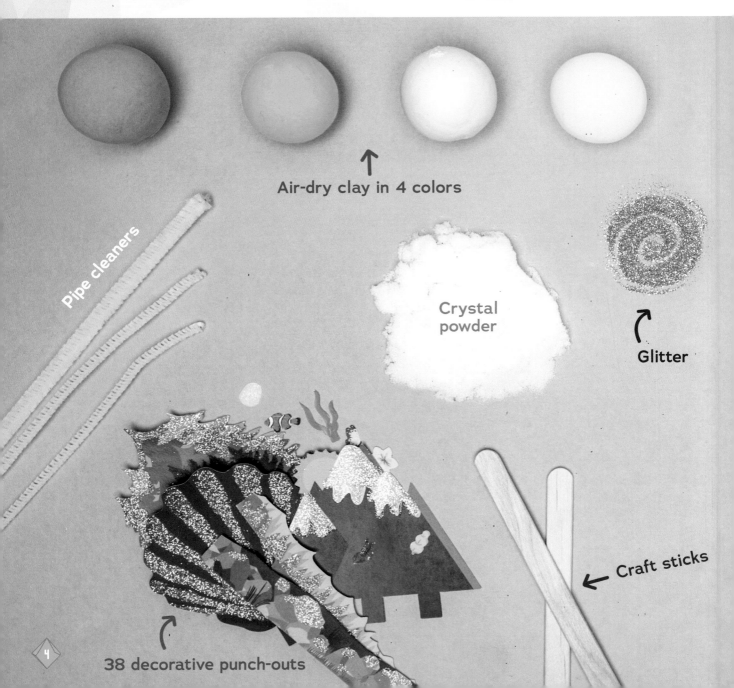

Air-dry clay in 4 colors

Pipe cleaners

Crystal powder

Glitter

38 decorative punch-outs

Craft sticks

4

Glue

Dye tablets in 4 colors

Nylon thread

3 mini figurines

3 display stands

Small heatproof jars with lids, about 10 fl oz (296 mL)

Measuring cup and spoons

Small pot

Distilled water

Metal spoon (for crafting only)

Potholder, trivet, and kitchen towel

Small plastic plate or lid

Plastic wrap

Scrap paper

School glue

Masking tape and clear tape

Pencil or marker

Rubber bands

High-quality clear nail polish

Optional: Coffee filter

How This BOOK WORKS

The supplies that come with this book will let you make three sparkling crystal scenes. To get the most of out of your projects, plan ahead! Consider this your master plan when making mini worlds.

STEP 1: PLAN AHEAD

Flip through the projects on pages 21–39 and read through the instructions and ideas. **Now it's time to make the following five Important Creative Decisions.**

Which theme?

Which figurine?

What kind of decorations?

What will the shape and color of my crystal be?

Which display?

STEP 2: GROW CRYSTALS

These crystals grow pretty quickly (see pages 13–16), but they need a bit of drying time. So plan on making the crystals over a day or two.

STEP 3: MAKE DECORATIONS

You can make decorations out of air-dry clay and paper punch-outs. Make any clay decorations at least an hour before you start assembling mini worlds so they can dry. But if you want to keep things speedy, just use punch-outs.

STEP 4: BUILD YOUR DISPLAY

Turn to pages 44–47 to build your paper displays. It's best to build the stand beforehand in order to make sure your mini world fits inside.

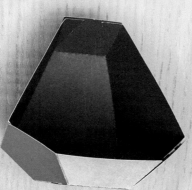

STEP 5: TIME TO CRAFT!

Now that everything is ready, you're ready to build your mini world! Follow the directions on the project pages to make the mini world of your dreams.

PLANNING TIPS

▸▸ **Your crystal growing solution is meant to be reused, so don't throw it out!** You may be able to use it two or three times depending on the size of the crystals that you grow.

▸▸ If you're growing a white crystal for any of your projects, plan on growing it first. You can add dye to the crystal solution later to make a colored crystal.

▸▸ Be sure to store any leftover air-dry clay in a resealable plastic baggie so it doesn't dry out.

Crafting TIPS

Keep these tips and tricks in mind while you're crafting.

IT'S ALWAYS A GOOD IDEA TO...

► Read the instructions before you start, follow them, and keep them handy so you can look things up when you need to. Only stick to the projects and crafts in this book.

► Wash your hands before and after you craft. Clean hands will also help your clay stay smudge-free.

► Keep food and drinks away from your crafting and crystal-growing areas. Don't grow crystals in areas where you eat or sleep, like the kitchen or bedroom.

► The projects in this book are only for readers ages 8 and up. Keep your supplies away from little kids and pets.

► Clean up and put away your supplies when you're done crafting. Wash any jars and utensils and wipe down any work surfaces.

WHILE YOU GROW CRYSTALS...

RECRUIT AN ADULT. An adult will need to supervise the crystal-growing part of your projects. The adult will also handle the stove, boiling water, and hot stuff. Have your adult read the instructions, too.

CHOOSE A GOOD WORKSPACE. For crystal growing, it's best to use a solid table that's heat resistant, which means it's OK to put hot things on it. The table should be somewhere with a constant temperature, so choose a place away from sunny windows.

PROTECT AGAINST SPILLS. Put down newspaper or paper towels on your table, and keep a trivet or potholder handy for hot jars. Since the dye can stain, wear old clothes or an apron and roll up your sleeves.

KEEP SEPARATE TOOLS. Use jars and utensils that are only for crystal growing—don't eat or drink from them afterward. Do not use drinking glasses to grow crystals.

WORKING WITH AIR-DRY CLAY...

KEEP DRYING TIME IN MIND. Small clay decorations usually dry within an hour or two. Let the clay bases for your mini worlds dry overnight.

STORE THE CLAY in an airtight storage bag after you open it, otherwise it will dry out. Try to squeeze the extra air out of the bag before you close it.

IF YOUR CLAY DRIES OUT, add a few drops of water to it. Knead the wet clay until it softens up. If the clay feels too wet, leave it out to dry for a few minutes.

IF YOU RUN OUT OF AIR-DRY CLAY, you can pick up more from your local crafts store.

Lab SAFETY

Read these guidelines before you start growing crystals.

WORKING WITH CRYSTAL POWDER & SOLUTIONS

▶ To open the crystal powder packet, cut along the dotted line at the top with scissors. Make sure you cut above the resealable lock on the bag. Don't use your teeth to open the packet!

▶ Keep the crystal powder, growing solution, and crystals away from your eyes, nose, and mouth.

▶ Don't let crystal powder or growing solution come into contact with the skin. If powder or growing solution does come in contact with your skin, clean the area with soap and water.

▶ To dispose of crystals, throw solid crystals and powders in the trash. Pour liquid solution directly into the sink drain.

DYE TABLETS

▶ Be careful when using the dye tablets since they may cause stains that won't wash out of fabrics. Cover your work surface and wear old clothes or an apron.

▶ Grow crystals away from furniture and carpets that you don't want to accidentally stain.

HANDLING HOT STUFF

► Only adults should heat liquids and handle hot jars and utensils. Do not leave the stove unattended while heating water or growing solution. Remember to turn off stove burners when you're done using them.

► When reheating growing solution, leave the jar open. Never use a microwave to heat water, seeding solution, or growing solution.

► Use a potholder or kitchen towel to handle hot jars. Always place hot jars on a trivet or potholder to cool.

► Let hot jars cool slowly at room temperature. Do not put jars in the refrigerator or in the freezer to cool them.

► Remember: Steam is very hot! Avoid contact with steam since it may cause burns. Also avoid inhaling any steam or vapors from hot growing solution.

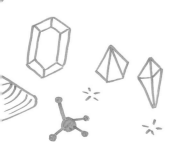   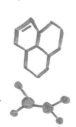  

Growing
CRYSTALS

YOU'LL NEED TO MAKE TWO KINDS OF SOLUTION FOR YOUR CRYSTALS.

Seeding solution forms tiny, microscopic crystals that help jump-start larger crystals.

Growing solution is what you'll use to grow large crystals.

Choose your project first (pages 21–39), then flip back here to make the solutions.

START WITH SEEDING SOLUTION

Seed pipe cleaners the **night before** you plan to grow your projects. You can even seed all your projects ahead of time to get the most out of your solution.

• WHAT YOU'LL NEED •

- 🔹 Masking tape
- 🔹 Pencil
- 🔹 Heatproof glass jars with lids (around 10 fl oz/296 mL)
- 🔹 Measuring spoon
- 🔹 Crystal powder
- 🔹 Small pot
- 🔹 Measuring cup
- 🔹 Distilled water
- 🔹 Trivet, potholder, and kitchen towel
- 🔹 Metal spoon
- 🔹 Small plastic plate or lid
- 🔹 Plastic wrap
- 🔹 Rubber band
- 🔹 An adult assistant
- 🔹 Optional: Coffee filter

1 Label a small heatproof glass jar with "seeding solution" and the date using masking tape. Add 1 tablespoon (15 g) of crystal powder to the jar and place it on a potholder or trivet.

2 Have your adult assistant boil ¼ cup (59 mL) of distilled water. Turn off the stove and let it cool for 30 seconds. Then have your assistant pour the hot water into the jar with the powder.

3 Stir the solution with the spoon until all the powder dissolves. Have your adult assistant put the lid on. Let the jar cool for about 5 minutes so that the solution is still warm, but not hot.

4 Prep your pipe cleaner according to the project instructions. Open the jar and stir the solution. Dip the pipe cleaner so that it's totally soaked.

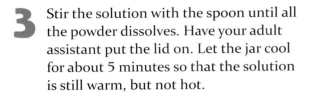

5 Lay your pipe cleaner on a plastic plate or lid. Let it dry completely (overnight is best). Close your seeding solution jar and save it for future projects.

6 After the pipe cleaner is completely dry, tiny crystals should become visible on the fibers. This means the pipe cleaner has been seeded. If not, reheat the seeding solution (page 17) and repeat Steps 4 and 5 on this page.

KNOW YOUR H$_2$O While the water that comes out of your tap is probably fine for drinking, it may contain minerals that aren't great for crystal growing. Distilled water is purified, so that's why it's recommended for these projects. You can buy distilled water at the grocery store or drugstore—check the label to make sure it says that it's purified by distillation.

GROWING SOLUTION

Growing solution is what you'll use to grow the crystals in your projects. It's best to mix up the solution **1 hour before** you plan to grow your crystals to get the temperature right.

1 Label the jar with your project name and the date. It's best if your jar holds about 10 fl oz (296 mL). Add 4 tablespoons (60 g) of crystal powder into the jar and place it on a potholder or trivet.

2 Have your assistant boil 1 cup (237 mL) of distilled water. Let it stand for 30 seconds, then have your assistant pour the hot water into the jar with the powder.

3 Stir the solution until all the powder dissolves completely. There shouldn't be any powder visible in the solution. If you'd like to add dye (page 20), add it now.

4 Have your assistant put the lid on the jar. Let the jar cool for at least 1 hour. You want the solution to be just a little warm (about 100°F or 38°C) before you grow crystals in it.

5 Place the seeded pipe cleaner shape into the solution and put the craft stick across the jar's mouth. Wind the thread around the craft stick so that the shape hangs in the center of the solution.

6 Cover the jar's mouth with plastic wrap and secure it with a rubber band. Over the next 2–4 hours, crystals will start to form on the pipe cleaner. Try not to bump or move the jar.

7 When the pipe cleaner is covered with crystals, remove it from the solution. Hang it in an empty jar to let it dry. Once it's dry, paint on two coats of clear nail polish to keep the color bright, otherwise the crystal will turn white over time.

TIP

If you're done growing crystals, keep your leftover solution in a tightly sealed jar. Follow the directions on the next page to reuse it for future projects.

If you're having trouble growing crystals, check out page 48 for some troubleshooting tips.

USING LEFTOVER SOLUTION

You can use leftover solution once or twice, depending on the size of the crystals you grow. Use up your solution within two weeks of making it, or throw it out.

1 Remove the lid from your jar and place it into a pot filled with a few inches of tap water.

Your assistant should slowly heat the water in the pot so that it simmers (not boiling) to gently heat the solution in the jar.

3 Have your assistant stir the solution as it heats up. He or she should break up any crystals on the bottom of the jar with the spoon.

4 Once all the crystals have dissolved, your assistant should remove the jar from the pot and place it on a kitchen towel. Have your assistant place the lid on, and let the jar cool for at least an hour until it's just warm (100°F or 38°C).

FILTERING LEFTOVER SOLUTION

Dust and dirt in your solution will cause crystals to form randomly (and not on the pipe cleaner). Check to see if your leftover solution is clean, but if not, place a coffee filter over the mouth of a clean jar and put a rubber band over the mouth to secure it. After you've reheated the seeding or growing solution, pour it through the filter to strain out any dust particles.

Crystal
SCIENCE

Wondering how you'll transform plain old powder into a glittery crystal world? Check these pages out for the science behind this sparkly craft.

WHAT IS A CRYSTAL?

A **crystal** is any solid in which the atoms and molecules have arranged themselves into a repeating pattern. The repeating pattern makes the crystal grow in a certain shape.

HOW DO MY CRYSTALS GROW?

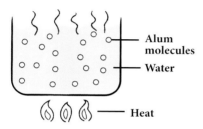

Alum molecules — Water — Heat

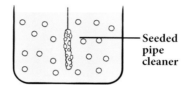

Seeded pipe cleaner

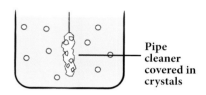

Pipe cleaner covered in crystals

To grow crystals, you'll dissolve alum powder into very hot water to create a liquid growing solution. Heating up the water causes the molecules to move faster and allows more alum molecules into the water. You can mix more alum powder into hot water than you could if the water was at room temperature. This extra alum makes this solution supersaturated.

Once the crystal powder is dissolved, the alum molecules float around freely so they can bond together to make crystals. You'll let the growing solution cool a little, and then put in a pipe cleaner shape that you've grown tiny alum crystals on beforehand (pages 13–14).

As the growing solution cools, the alum molecules will be attracted to the tiny crystals on your pipe cleaner and will bond to them, making the crystals grow bigger. Eventually the crystals will cover the pipe cleaner.

WHAT'S IN MY CRYSTAL POWDER? Your crystal powder is made of the chemical **aluminum potassium sulfate**, also called alum for short. Alum is mined from mineral deposits found in the earth. Along with making crystals, alum has many other uses, like purifying water, putting the crunch in pickle recipes, and as an ingredient in deodorants.

Dyeing CRYSTALS

Your kit comes with four dye tablets to make a rainbow of crystal colors. Here's how to use them.

CRYSTAL COLOR	DYE TABLETS TO ADD
Pink	1 red
Peach	1 red + 1 yellow
Yellow	1 yellow
Mint	1 yellow + ½ blue
Aqua	1 blue
Purple	1 purple

1 Choose the color you want from the chart on the right and gather the tablets you need. If you need to, cut tablets with a butter knife on a piece of paper (to catch the crumbs).

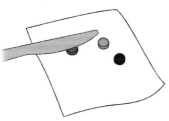

2 Add the tablets to the hot growing solution after you've dissolved the crystal powder in Step 3 on page 16.

project 96

COLOR TIPS

▶ As soon as your crystals dry, **paint on two coats of high-quality clear nail polish** to prevent the color from fading. If you don't glaze your crystal, it may fade over time.

▶ You can also use **liquid food coloring** to color your crystals. About 20–25 drops of food coloring usually makes a nice color.

▶ As crystals grow, they try to attract only other alum molecules, so this may make the color uneven. But don't worry—**color streaks make your crystals unique**.

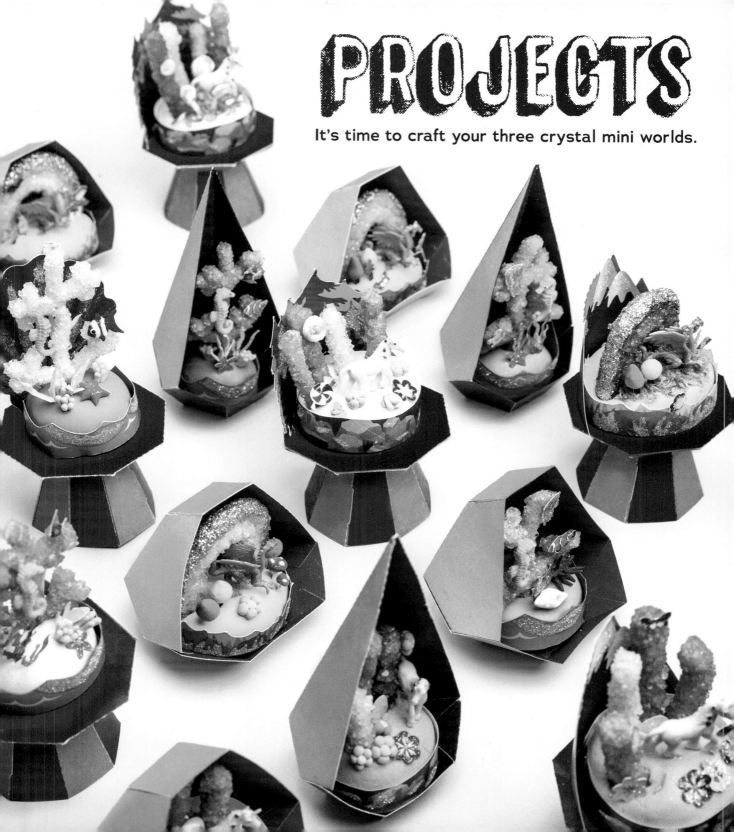

PROJECTS

It's time to craft your three crystal mini worlds.

Crystal Coral Reef

Dive under the sea with this sparkly coral reef.

• WHAT YOU'LL NEED •

- ✷ Thin pipe cleaners
- ✷ Scissors
- ✷ Crystal-growing supplies (pages 13–16)
- ✷ Craft stick
- ✷ Nylon thread
- ✷ Tape
- ✷ Clear nail polish
- ✷ Air-dry clay
- ✷ Sea horse figurine
- ✷ Punch-outs
- ✷ Display stand (pages 44–47)
- ✷ Glue

1 Cut your thin pipe cleaners into the following size pieces shown below:

**1 inch
(2.5 cm)**

**¾ inch
(2 cm)
(4 pieces)**

**1 ½ inches
(4 cm)**

**2 ½ inches
(6.5 cm)**

2 Twist the 1- and 1½-inch pipe cleaner pieces around the longest piece to form branches. Then twist the ¾-inch pieces around the branch ends to make twigs.

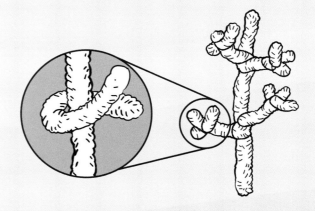

23

3 Cut a 6-inch (15 cm) piece of nylon thread. Tie one end to the stem of the pipe cleaner branch, and cut the tail of the knot short. Tape the other end of the thread to a craft stick.

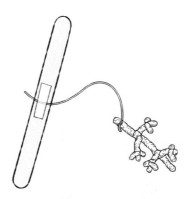

4 Follow the directions on pages 13–16 to seed and grow crystals on your pipe cleaner branch. Once the crystal is dry, coat it twice with clear nail polish to keep the colors bright.

5 If you'd like to add clay seaweed or sea sponges (pages 26–27), make them now and let them dry. Choose and build your display stand from pages 44–47.

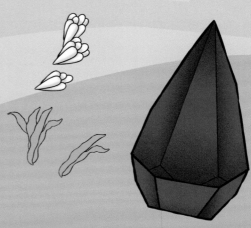

6 Decide where you want the sea horse and paper punch-outs on your crystal. Lay the crystal flat, and use a dab of glue to attach them to the crystal. Let it dry.

TIP If you want your sea horse to rest on the clay base, you can glue it to the base after the clay dries.

7 Roll a ball of clay about 1½ inches wide. Use the circle below to help you measure.

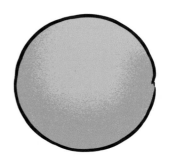

8 Take the crystal branch and press the stem into the base so that the branch stands up.

If you'd like to skip the display stand, just add a large seashell punch-out behind the coral branch in Step 9 on page 26.

9 Add any clay decorations and paper punch-outs you'd like to the clay base. Just press them into the clay.

TIP

You can snip off a little of the bottom of dry sea sponge clusters and seaweed to create a flat bottom. This might make decorating a little easier.

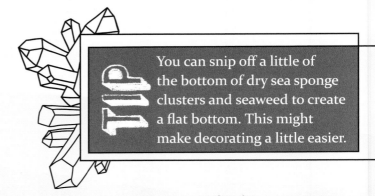

Decorate with Clay

SEA SPONGES

1 Start with a tiny ball of clay.

2 Press lightly on one side of the ball and roll it against the table to make a long teardrop.

3 Make a few more long teardrops. Stick them together to form a cluster. Let it dry.

10 Place the mini world into the paper stand to see that it fits, then take it out. Let everything dry. (If you leave the wet base in the stand to dry, it may stick to the display.)

11 After the clay dries, you can wrap the paper border around the base and glue it in place before you put the mini world into the display. Done!

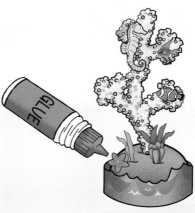

SEAWEED

1 Take a tiny bit of clay and roll a thin snake.

2 Press lightly on the snake to make a leaf shape.

3 To create a ruffled edge, gently pull on the ends to stretch the leaf.

4 Make more leaves and bundle them together at one end. Let the leaf bundle dry.

DAZZLING
DRAGON'S LAIR

Build a glittering crystal cave for your fierce mini dragon.

1 Take the thick pipe cleaner and crumple it up so it has bends and kinks. Fold the pipe cleaner into a thick arch about 1 ½ inches (4 cm) wide.

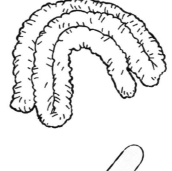

2 Cut a 6-inch (15 cm) piece of nylon thread. Tie one end to the pipe cleaner arch and cut the tail of the knot short. Tape the other end of the thread to a craft stick.

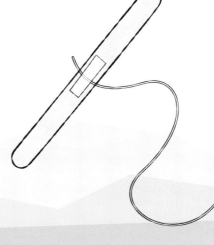

3 Follow the directions on pages 13–16 to seed and grow crystals on your pipe cleaner arch. Once the crystal is dry, coat it twice with clear nail polish to keep the color bright.

4 Pour the silver glitter onto a piece of scrap paper in a small pile. Add a layer of school glue to the outside of the crystal arch. Dip the wet glue of the arch in glitter, and let it dry.

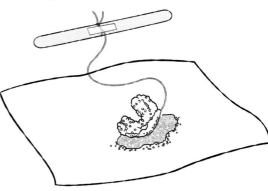

TIP
You can use the glue that comes with this book to add glitter, but school glue works the best.

5 If you'd like to seal in the glitter, add another coat of clear nail polish.

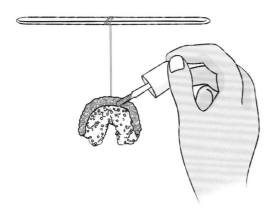

6 If you want to add clay decorations (pages 32–33), make them and let them dry before you start making your mini world. Choose and build your display stand from pages 44–47.

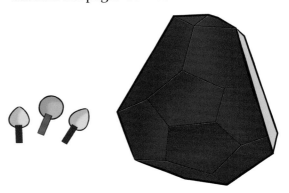

7 Roll a ball of clay about 1 ½ inches wide. Use the circle below to help you measure.

8 Take the crystal arch and press the ends into the base so that the arch stands up. Decide where you want the dragon and press its feet into the clay, too.

9 Add any clay decorations and paper punch-outs you'd like. Attach any decorations onto the crystal with the glue that comes with this book.

10 Place the mini world into the stand to make sure that it fits. Take the mini world out and let it dry. (If you leave the wet base in the stand to dry, it may stick to the display.)

DECORATE WITH CLAY

TREES

1 Press on one side of a tiny ball of clay. Gently roll it against the table to make a cone.

2 Insert a brown stick from your punch-out sheet into the bottom of the cone to make a tree.

11 After the clay dries, you can wrap the paper border around the base and glue it in place before you put the mini world into the display. Done!

3 To make a round tree, slightly flatten a tiny ball and insert a brown stick punch-out.

CLAY COLORS

You can mix the air-dry clay to make new colors. Below are a few shades that you might need.

● + ○	Peach
○ + ●	Green
● + ●	Purple

Rainbow Valley

Grow a cluster of fantastic crystals for this dreamy mini world.

This is a great project to make with leftover growing solution.

• WHAT YOU'LL NEED •

- Thin pipe cleaners
- Scissors
- Crystal-growing supplies (pages 13–16)
- Craft sticks
- Nylon thread
- Tape
- Air-dry clay
- Unicorn figurine
- Punch-outs
- Display stand (pages 44–47)
- Glue
- Optional: Pencil

1 Cut three or four pieces of thin pipe cleaner 1½ inches (4 cm) long.

2 For each crystal color, cut 6 inches (15 cm) of nylon thread. Tie one end to the pipe cleaner piece and cut the tail of the knot off. Tape the other end of the thread to a craft stick. If you'd like to grow two crystal sticks at once, tie the second pipe cleaner piece about 1½ inches above the first on the nylon thread.

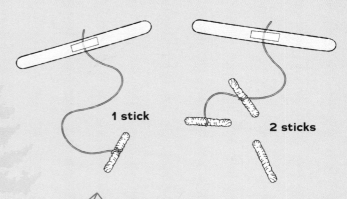

1 stick

2 sticks

TIP You might need to grow the crystals in multiple batches, so plan on an extra day or two for Step 3 on page 36.

3 Follow the directions on pages 13–16 to seed and grow crystals on your pipe cleaners. Once the crystals are dry, coat them twice with clear nail polish to keep the colors bright.

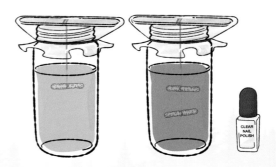

4 If you'd like to add clay decorations (pages 38–39), make them and let them dry before you start making your mini world. Choose and build a display stand from pages 44–47.

5 Roll a ball of clay about 1 ½ inches wide. Use the circle here to help you measure.

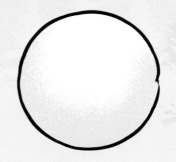

6 Press the unicorn figurine's feet into the clay so it stands up. Use the point of a pencil to help push the feet into the clay, if you need to.

7 Push your crystal sticks into the clay around the unicorn. Smooth over any bumps in the clay.

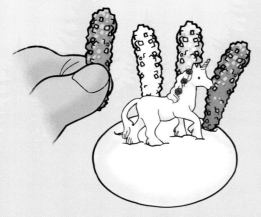

8 Add any paper punch-outs and clay decorations you'd like. Attach them onto the crystal or clay with glue.

9 Place the mini world onto the stand to make sure that it fits. Take the mini world out and let it dry. (If you leave the wet base on the stand to dry, it may stick to the display.)

Decorate with Clay

LOLLIPOP

1 Roll two thin snakes out of air-dry clay in two different colors. Each snake should be thinner than a toothpick.

2 Gently twist the two snakes together. Pinch the ends so that the clay stays twisted.

3 Coil the twist to make the lollipop. Push the end underneath the coil to hide it.

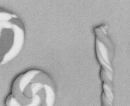

10 After the clay dries, you can wrap the paper border around the base and glue it in place before you put the mini world onto the display. Done!

TIP

If your mini world falls off its display, use a dab of glue to stick it permanently to the stand.

PEPPERMINT STICK

4 Carefully poke in a white stick punch-out into the coil to create a lollipop on a stick.

To make a peppermint stick, follow Steps 1 and 2 to make a twist and then let it dry completely. Use scissors to snip the dry twist into smaller sticks.

MORE IDEAS FOR YOUR WORLDS

Use craft supplies from home to make your worlds one-of-a-kind.

Place your mini world in a hanging ornament and use store-bought figurines.

Use your supplies to build a mini world inside a small gift box lid.

A seashell makes a fun base for your coral reef.

↓

Bury the base of your mini world in layers of colored sand.

↑

Make a dragon hatchling by using a mini plastic egg as a display stand.

Look for tiny containers, like this mini flowerpot, to hold your crystals.

SWEET SHAPES

If you're feeling adventurous, bend and twist your pipe cleaners in different shapes to create unique crystals. Here are some ideas to try.

Try using food coloring (page 20) to dye a crystal.

Coil a thick pipe cleaner into a crystal geode.

Make a straight stem to help your crystal stand up in the clay base.

Thin pipe cleaners work best for delicate shapes.

Love music?
Try a treble clef.

Wrap the
pipe cleaner
around a pencil
to create a
perfect spiral.

Make your favorite lucky
charm, like this clover.

Making Your DISPLAYS

For all your paper stands, you should first punch them out of the white sheet. Then fold the stands along the score lines. (They're the lines that are pressed into the paper.) The dark solid color goes on the inside of each stand.

PINK PEDESTAL

1 Fold the two pink pieces along the score lines. Spread glue on tab A and press it so that it lines up with the matching letter on the dark pink underside.

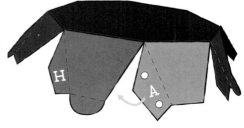

2 Glue on tabs B–H to their matching letters to make a platform. The underside should look like the picture below.

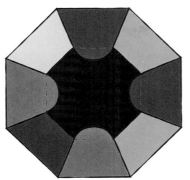

3 Fold the half-circle flaps out.

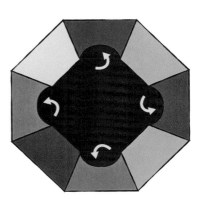

4 For the fan-shaped piece, spread glue on the light pink edge and insert tab I into the slot to form the base cone.

5 Insert each half-circle flap on the platform into a slit in the base cone. (The color stripes on the platform and base aren't supposed to match.)

6 To add a background punch-out, slide the tabs of the punch-out into the slits in the platform.

TIP

Hold the glued flaps together with your fingers until they stick.

1 Fold the stand along the score lines. For tabs A–E, spread glue on the tab and press it to the matching letter on the dark purple underside. Go in alphabet order.

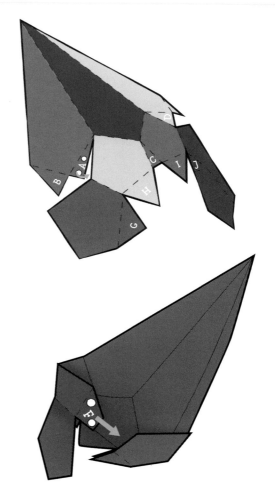

2 Glue tab F to the matching letter on the dark purple underside to close the lip of your stand.

3 Spread glue on tabs G–J and fold the pentagon flap over them all at once.

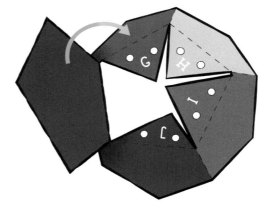

1 Fold the stand along the score lines. For tabs A–E, spread glue on the tab and press it to the matching letter on the dark blue underside. Glue the tabs in alphabet order.

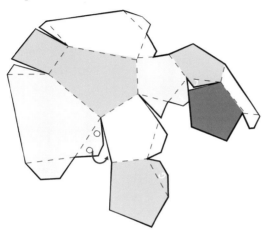

2 Glue tab F to the matching letter on the dark blue underside to close the lip of your stand.

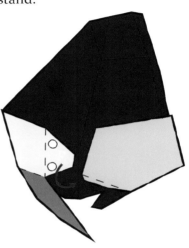

3 Spread glue on tabs G–J and fold the pentagon flap over them all at once.

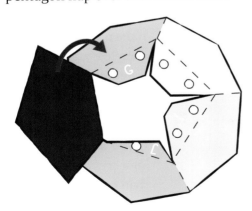

4 Spread glue on tabs K and L and fold the square flap over them to finish.

TROUBLESHOOTING

Are those pesky crystals giving you trouble? Read on for some solutions to common crystal-growing problems.

MY CRYSTALS WON'T GROW.

Check these three things:

▸ Check that you're seeding the pipe cleaners properly (pages 13–14). You should see tiny crystals in the fibers—if you don't see any, repeat the seeding.

▸ Wait for the growing solution to cool before you put the seeded pipe cleaner inside. If the solution is too hot, then you might accidentally dissolve your seed crystals.

▸ If you still don't have any crystals, try leaving the crystal in longer and leaving the jar open. This lets the solution evaporate, which will form a crystal slowly over a few days.

CRYSTALS ARE GROWING ON THE BOTTOM OF THE JAR, NOT ON THE PIPE CLEANER.

Sometimes dust and other particles can get into your growing solution and cause crystals to grow randomly. Turn to page 17 and follow the instructions for filtering.

MY CRYSTAL GREW INTO A BOULDER!

Be sure to keep an eye on your crystal while it grows, and pull it out when the crystals just cover the pipe cleaner. If the crystal is really too big, you can try scraping some off, but you might have to start from scratch.

I THINK I MIXED THE GROWING SOLUTION WRONG.

▸ **If you added too much powder:** If the powder won't dissolve completely, add a little more hot water. Watch the crystal as it grows—it may form faster than normal.

▸ **If you added too little powder:** Your crystals might take longer than normal to form. Unseal the jar and put a coffee filter on top of the opening to let the solution evaporate over a day or two.